IT'S A GREAT WALL!

IT'S A GREAT WALL!

WATSON-GUPTILL PUBLICATIONS / NEW YORK

Pictures and Text by
Michael Webb & Arnold Schwartzman

Copyright © 2000, by The Images Publishing Group Pty Ltd
6 Bastow Place, Mulgrave, Victoria 3170, Australia

Published in the United States in 2000 by
Watson-Guptill Publications,
a division of BPI Communications, Inc.
1515 Broadway, New York, NY 10036

Book design: The Graphic Image Studio Pty Ltd, Mulgrave, Australia

Library of Congress Cataloging-in-Publication Data for this title
can be obtained by writing to the Library of Congress, Washington,
D.C. 20540

ISBN 0-8230-2169-6

Printed in Hong Kong
1 2 3 4 5 6 7 8 9 / 07 06 05 04 03 02 01 00

Contents

Introduction

Every wall has two sides, and more than one role.
Robert Frost anticipated the inglorious history of the
Berlin Wall when he wrote, in 1914:

'Before I built a wall I'd ask to know

What I was walling in or walling out

And to whom I was like to give offense.

Something there is that doesn't love a wall,

That wants it down.'

Gun battery at Longues, Normandy: part of the Nazis' Atlantic Wall [1]

Fragments of celebrated
walls embedded in the 'wall
of walls' at the Chicago
Tribune, Chicago [2]

Trailer with walled-up rear window [5]

Walls are the building blocks of our homes and cities, the barriers we erect to protect our lives and property. They are so obvious that we take them for granted—though few experiences are more comforting than the shelter of stout walls on a stormy night. Some walls have greater significance. They were raised to define the boundaries of empires, and to enclose great cities. Rulers constructed high-walled castles to defend their domains and intimidate their subjects. No prospect was more terrifying to the Allied soldiers on D-Day than the Nazis' Atlantic wall with its fortified bunkers spewing fire. Now, these massive concrete gun emplacements have joined the relics of former tyrants as enduring memorials of bravery and brutality. Grand or humble, ancient or modern, each of the walls illustrated here tells us something about the time and place in which it was built.

Krak des Chevaliers, Syria—a 12th-century Crusader fortress [4]

Memorial to Stonewall Jackson on the Manassas
battlefield, Virginia [5]

Walls can also function as metaphors. When the rustics
of Shakespeare's *A Midsummer Night's Dream* play the
'lamentable comedy of Pyramus and Thisbe,' the Prologue
introduces Snout: 'This man with lime and roughcast doth
present/Wall, that vile Wall which did these lovers sunder.'
'Stone walls do not a prison make,' wrote the English
cavalier poet Richard Lovelace, as his spirit soared to
embrace his beloved Althea. 'There stands Jackson like
a stone wall,' observed a Confederate officer as a brigadier
rallied his troops at the first battle of Bull Run. The nickname
stuck, and Jackson went on to win acclaim as one of the
finest generals of the American Civil War. 'Walls have ears,'
declared posters that urged the population to beware of
spies in the second world war. Evelyn Neff, a psychologist
practicing in Washington DC, tells her patients to think of
their personal barriers as walls that can be surmounted,
circumvented, or torn down.

Playing deck tennis
against a seaborne wall
on the SS Norway [7]

Serendipity can play a role. Eighteenth-century
convicts at the Fleet prison in London had plenty
of time but little elbow-room. To amuse themselves
they hit a ball against the walls with a wooden
paddle, and this evolved into the games of squash
racquets and handball at England's most exclusive
public schools and clubs. The Eton Wall Game
began as a local version of football adapted to
a strip of grass, 120 yds x 6 yds, bordering
a brick wall. The goals were a door at one end
and a tree at the other, and the game remains
unique to its site. In contrast, the defensive wall
that soccer players form to block opponents'
penalty kicks has flourished worldwide since
a lighter ball was introduced in the 1960s.

The word 'wall' derives from old English and the Latin *vallum* (rampart). The Shorter Oxford English Dictionary offers almost a page of definitions which indicate an extraordinary versatility: wall of silence, backs to the wall, to drive to the wall, drive up the wall, off the wall, go over the wall (in prison slang), talk to a brick wall, wall newspaper, wall-to-wall are a few of the uses. The French *mur*, German *mauer*, and Italian *muro* all derive from the Latin *murus*—from which we get 'mural.' The French movie director Agnes Varda made a documentary about the wall artists of Venice, California, which she titled *Mur-Murs*.

Superimposed lettering on a wall in South Street Seaport, New York [8]

Fragment of the medieval ramparts framed by a modern wall in Genoa, Italy [10]

Portuguese ramparts protect the Moslem city of Essaouira, Morocco [9]

Shadow cast on a decaying wall in Tonantzintla, Mexico [11]

Stone trees support a
promenade in Antoni Gaudi's
Parc Guell, Barcelona [12]

This anthology of walls around the world is divided into four overlapping categories: Symbolism, Protection, Materials, and Ornament. Some walls are born as symbols—of power or celebration; others, like the Western Wall in Jerusalem, have greatness thrust upon them. Walls that were fiercely contested become objects of nostalgia. 'The splendour falls on castle walls,' wrote Alfred Lord Tennyson in an era that romanticized the age of chivalry. Other eye-catching walls were built to trick or delight the eye, and some of the most beautiful were designed simply to clear rocky fields and enclose livestock. Beauty of materials or patterning may be there from the start, or be added—by a mural painter or the chance effects of decay.

Symbolism

*'Mountain clouds like chairmen
bear the Great Wall from the sea,'*
wrote the Chinese poet Tsu Yung,
12 centuries ago.

The wall was already a thousand years old. Shih Huang Ti, who proclaimed himself the first emperor of China and united its warring provinces, consolidated existing barriers, using forced labor to create a wall that snaked 1,500 miles over mountain and desert, was studded with 25,000 towers, and was broad enough to allow five horsemen to gallop abreast along its parapet. Repeatedly abandoned and rebuilt, it failed to block nomadic invaders, but served—along with the ocean and the mountain ranges to the south and east— as a symbolic boundary of the empire, a line of demarcation between civilization and barbarism.

Today, every VIP who visits Beijing is driven out to a meticulously restored section of this fragmented monument, which took its present form during the Ming dynasty, about 400 years ago. 'It's a *great* wall,' declared President Nixon on his historic visit to restore US-Chinese ties. A banal comment, but it was bound to please his hosts. However, the wall

An elaborately preserved section of the
Great Wall of China near Beijing [14]

is a lot less impressive for most of its course, and the earth ramparts have melted away into the soil. Two parallel segments of the wall were identified in radar photographs taken from the space shuttle Endeavor, but it's a myth that the wall could be glimpsed by the astronauts who landed on the moon.

Through the centuries of imperial rule, every walled Chinese town had its statue of Ch'eng-huang, the god of walls and ditches, and the same symbol 城 was used for both walls and cities. Walls provided defense against warlords and evil spirits, and maintained a strict social hierarchy. The imperial capital of Beijing resembled a set of boxes, one inside the other, with the emperor at the center of the innermost enclosure.

Balustrades in the courtyard of Beijing's Forbidden City—a Chinese box of walls [15]

Lion Gate, Mycenae (Greece), which leads to the legendary acropolis of Agamemnon [16]

Poetry and symbol loomed large in other ancient cultures. The Incas and Agamemnon's builders used stones that were much larger than they needed to be, awing their subjects and giving birth to legends about a race of giants. At the very birth of urban civilization, the rulers of Mesopotamia built ziggurats that would reunite earth and sky, and commissioned massive, richly ornamented walls. The Ishtar Gate and the ceramic encrusted walls that flanked it can now be seen in Berlin's Pergamon Museum.

Assyrian ceramic relief on the wall leading to the Ishtar Gate of Babylon [17]

Twelve-sided Inca stone on Hatunrumiyok Street in Cuzco, Peru [18]

The Old Testament is full of stories about walled cities that came to a bad end. Joshua tells how the Lord instructed the Israelites to march around Jericho, blowing rams horns, for six days. On the seventh day, 'when the people heard the sound of the trumpet, and the people shouted with a great shout, the wall fell down flat.' Archeologists excavating the ruins now conjecture that its wall did suddenly collapse in about 1400 BC, though probably as the result of an earthquake. Before he challenged the UN, Saddam Hussein was rebuilding the ruined walls of Babylon to forge a symbolic link between himself and Nebuchadnezzar, forgetting how the earlier tyrant reputedly went mad and ate grass.

تل السلطان

كم ١½

TELL SULTAN
OLD WALLS
OF JERICHO

Tourist marker in Jericho, Palestine [19]

City wall of Jerusalem to the south of the Jaffa Gate [20]

According to legend Jerusalem's Golden Gate will remain walled-up until Judgment Day [21]

Damascus Gate, the busiest of the seven entrances to the old city of Jerusalem [22]

Jerusalem is a city that is holy to three religions and its walls have resonated through the ages. For almost 4,000 years, its site has been contested and fortified by Egyptians and Israelites, Babylonians and Persians, Hellenes and Romans, Arabs, Crusaders and Ottomans. Medieval Christians portrayed it as the center of the world with a direct link to heaven. In 1917, when General Allenby took Jerusalem from the Turks, he followed the advice of the British War Office, which cabled him this message: "Strongly suggest dismounting at gate. German Emperor rode in and the saying went round, 'A better man than he walked.' Advantages of contrast will be obvious." Today visitors can promenade along a section of the ramparts, which were rebuilt for Suleyman the Magnificent on foundations that go back to Herod, gazing out to the golden rocks that surround the modern city, and looking down into the labyrinth of streets and courtyards within. The four quarters of the old city bustle with life and everyone has to enter through one of seven ancient gates. The eighth, the Golden Gate, will remain walled-up, according to tradition, until Judgment Day.

Ottoman tower on the north wall of Jerusalem [23]

For Jews, the most sacred site in the world is the Western Wall—
part of the retaining wall around the base of the Second Temple
which King Herod improved and the Romans destroyed—now that
the platform above has become a Moslem sanctuary. Eleven courses
of massive unmortared stones rise from a plaza that was cleared and
paved soon after Israeli troops repossessed the old city in the 1967
war. Bushes spout from crevices, and those within reach are stuffed
with handwritten prayers and requests. Above, are smaller stones
that were added over the centuries to patch what had tumbled and
to create a parapet. Nineteen original courses remain buried, and
most of the foundations are concealed behind old buildings and
the outer walls.

It is hard to convey the intensity of devotion these stones inspire,
and the central role they play in the life of every Israeli, native-born
and immigrant, orthodox to secular. Hassidim spend hours touching
and speaking to the stones;. The sick come to be healed, soldiers to
remember fallen comrades, and great crowds assemble on holy days
or at moments of national crisis. Michal Ronnen Safdie spent a year
photographing worshippers, from as close as she could get (men are
segregated from women) and from the terrace of the house that her
husband, Moshe Safdie, rebuilt at the edge of the Jewish Quarter.
Among the images in her book, *The Western Wall*, is a telescopic
view of Moslem worshippers prostrating themselves above, and
Jewish worshippers below, each unaware of the others' presence—
a poignant symbol of this divided city.

The Western Wall draws
crowds on holy days and
during national crises (24)

The Memorial de la
Deportation on the Ile
de la Cite in Paris [26]

Monument to the
French Resistance
of World War II in
Montmartre, Paris [27]

The execution wall of the Auschwitz concentration camp is now a memorial to the slain [28]

There is a spiritual link between Jerusalem's Western Wall and the memorials to victims of the Holocaust. In Cracow, Catholic students erected a wall of desecrated Jewish tombstones; at Auschwitz the wall of execution has become a shrine. In Paris, the Memorial de la Deportation occupies a sunken court at the eastern tip of the Ile de la Cite. High concrete walls border the narrow flights of steps that lead down to a simulated prison yard, from where you can see nothing but water and sky. Isolated from the world, you pass between two huge millstones into a chamber that commemorates the French victims of the Nazi death camps. The sense of isolation from the world, of walls moving in to crush you, is deeply affecting.

Jewish tombstones form a Holocaust memorial in Cracow, Poland [29]

Maya Lin employed a similar strategy of isolation and restraint in her fiercely contested competition-winning design for the Vietnam Veterans Memorial in Washington DC. In a town of white marble colonnades, high-flown inscriptions, and pompous statuary—a formula that is about to be recycled for the second world war monument—Lin pared her design to the essentials. A paved path leads down into an angled gash in the earth. The names of the dead are incised chronologically on two tapered walls of polished black granite panels, from the central divide to the eastern tip, and from the western extremity back to the center. Thus the first and last casualties of war are juxtaposed at the deepest point. Visitors are swallowed up in this symbolic grave, confronted with the enormity of the slaughter. Yet they can reach out and trace a single name, establishing direct contact with an individual. Reflections link the living to the dead; the world beneath the earth with the trees and sky. Lin was a 21-year-old student at Yale when she had her 'strong, sure vision,' and her wall has become a national shrine, healing the wounds left by this century's most divisive war.

(Above and right)
Maya Lin's Vietnam Veterans
Memorial, Washington DC (30, 31)

The grave site of John Fitzgerald Kennedy, looking over Washington DC [32]

Other memorials exploit the power of walls to arouse the emotions. President Kennedy's grave in Arlington National Cemetary, Washington DC, is flanked by a curved parapet inscribed with excerpts from his inaugural address which encloses a belvedere looking out over the city. Equally moving are the words of Robert Kennedy, inscribed on a neighboring memorial.

On Ellis Island in New York harbor, a wall of names celebrates a part of those huddled masses that passed through this immigration station on their way to a new life. The Astronauts Memorial at Cape Canaveral, designed by Holt Hinshaw Pfau Jones, comprises a wall of polished granite that rotates and tilts to face away from the sun. Pivoting mirrors reflect sunlight through the names of astronauts which are etched out of the stone.

In Berlin in 1926, Mies van der Rohe designed an Expressionist brick facade to recall the murder of the communist revolutionaries Karl Liebknecht and Rosa Luxemburg. The architect had criticized the first design as something more suitable for bankers, and chose this form because, as he remarked, 'most of these people were shot in front of a wall.' It was one of the first monuments the Nazis destroyed when they seized power in 1933.

Ellis Island immigrants memorial wall, New York [33]

Postman's Wall is one of the most eccentric and little-known treasures of London: a poignant expression of Victorian moral values, located next to a post office just east of the financial district. Inaugurated in 1900, this wall of ceramic plaques chronicles acts of selfless heroism by uncelebrated heroes.

For architects, the wall can be the focus of their design. Louis Kahn created buildings with the weight and authority of ancient ruins. Antoine Predock is inspired by the massive adobe walls of his native New Mexico, but he built a free-standing wall of mirrored glass to achieve a sense of place and ritual at a modest university

Salk Institute, La Jolla, California: Louis Kahn's monumental research center [34]

Postman's Park, a memorial wall to heroic deeds inaugurated in 1900 in East London [35]

theater on the San Diego campus of the University of California. James Wines designed peeling, tilting and crumbling facades for Best Company hardware stores, making them stand out in the plastic wilderness of suburban malls. Artists Claes Oldenburg and Coosje van Bruggen devised the image of a knife cutting through a plain stucco facade to identify an art gallery in West Hollywood.

Fine Arts Center of Arizona State University, Tempe, designed by Antoine Predock [36]

Antoine Predock's mirrored wall at the Mandell Weiss Forum Theater, La Jolla, California [37]

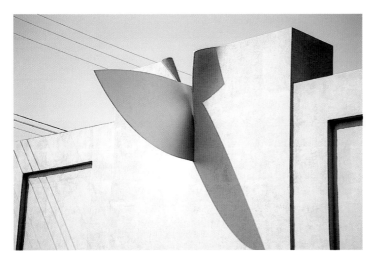

Margo Leavin Gallery, West Hollywood (Claes Oldenburg and Coosje van Bruggen) [38]

Dislocated facade of a Best Company store, Sacramento, California, designed by SITE Projects [39]

Some walls pretend to be something more than they are. The 'Jealous Wall' at Belvedere House in County Westmeath, Ireland, is a picturesque Gothic ruin that could easily be another of the follies that 18th-century landowners built to draw the eye to an enticing vista. This one was erected, at great expense, by the first Earl merely to block his view of the larger house that his brother George had built, a half mile away.

Crumbling facade of Best Company store, Houston, Texas [40]

(Right) The 'Jealous Wall' shut out the view of a brother's house in County Westmeath, Ireland [41]

No wall had more symbolic power than the one that sundered Berlin. From its hasty erection in August 1961, to its frenzied overthrow in November 1989, it imprisoned people on both sides. Thrown up overnight as a crude barrier to stem the mass flight of East Germans to the West, it was rebuilt three times to foil determined escapees. Its final version comprised a double layer of super-hard, rebar-reinforced concrete, 15 feet high and 103 miles long. To the East it was a lethal barrier, gray and unapproachable. Rabbits gamboled in the minefields but over 200 people were killed trying to cross the death strip. For the military, it was a potential flash-point; for Western politicians a rallying point for freedom. 'Democracy is not perfect, but we have never had to put a wall up to keep our people in,' declared Robert Kennedy. In 1987, President Reagan went further, appealing to Gorbachev to 'tear down this wall' and—to his and everyone's else's astonishment—the Soviets abandoned their client soon after that quixotic speech and the wall was torn down.

(Above and below) Breaking down the Berlin Wall in December 1989 [42, 44]

The Berlin Wall severed the Potsdamer Strasse [43]

Unsullied to the East, the Western face of the wall became a canvas for art and graffiti [45]

Fragments of Berlin wall in the German Pavilion at Expo '92, Seville [46]

Westerners climbed ladders to sightsee, and (from the early 1980s on) blanketed the wall with anarchic graffiti and art works, turning it into the world's largest canvas. Keith Haring did a signature piece, and there was a row of talking penises. *Berlin Wird Mauerfrei* ('Berlin will be free of walls') was one prophetic inscription. Once breached, the wall became an instant relic; its fragments peddled to tourists and exhibited in museums. Cartoonists had a field day; one portrayed Karl Marx as Humpty Dumpty falling in a tumble of blocks. Billions of marks have been spent to obliterate its trail and stitch the two halves of the city together. The wall is likely to live on only in memory as a psychological scar on the reunited city, a ghostly reminder of a catastrophe averted.

Protection

A t the dawn of human settlement, caves provided shelter from predators and the elements, but as soon as people moved out to farm the land, trade, and fight, their survival depended on walls. Rulers built castles and ramparts to protect their domains and flaunt their authority. But fortifications were often a demonstration of vulnerability as much as power. Mobile forces were the first line of defense for flourishing states. A wall protected the northern boundary of the Roman empire from Scots raiders, but Rome itself saw little need for static defenses until the barbarians were at its gates and by then it had rotted from within and offered little resistance to the Goths and Vandals.

The city of Rome still has its walls, reconstructed by the Emperor Aurelian in the 3rd-century, and constantly altered since then. A museum, the Museo delle Mure has been installed in the medieval towers of St Sebastian's gate, and from here visitors can walk along the ramparts and out onto the Appian Way. A more poignant relic of the Roman empire lies 1,300 miles north. Three legions and about 40,000 laborers worked from AD 122–25 to build Hadrian's Wall. It was an awesome undertaking. Bulwarks of rubble faced with local stone extended 80 miles across the narrow neck of England. There were mile-castles from which defenders could sally forth, and turrets for shelter every third of a mile. The wall averaged 15 feet high and about nine feet wide, and was rarely breached in its three centuries of use. The legionnaires had more to fear from cold and damp than the Scots. Restored fragments are scattered across expanses of windswept pasture, but most of the wall has been pillaged for building stone or grassed over.

(Above and right) Hadrian's Wall
protected the northern boundary of the
Roman empire from the Scots [47, 48]

Gate of Domme, a *bastide* (fortified town) of 1281 in the Dordogne region of France (50)

In the centuries that followed the *Pax Romana*, power was concentrated behind castle walls, and life outside was nasty, brutish, and short. Not until the 11th-century did bishops and feudal lords begin to fortify towns to defend their domains, and thus create secure containers that became magnets for trade and generators of wealth. Walls defined cities and won them charters, and city deities were often portrayed with mural crowns. During the turbulent 13th-century, *bastides* (fortified towns) were built by French and English kings to encourage settlement along disputed borders in the region of Aquitaine. Domme, in the Dordogne was one; another, built to protect the troops of St Louis as they embarked for the seventh Crusade in 1248, is Aigues-Mortes. Their plans are as basic as those of Roman camps: a grid of streets within a square of walls, and a massive church that doubled as look-out tower and *donjon* beside a central market square.

(Above and below) Coca Castle, Castile, Spain: a 14th-century stronghold that was built for show [52, 53]

Walls were often built more for show than strength, as a demonstration of civic pride and prosperity, like a great square or church. Fancy-dress fortifications—like those of Coca Castle in Castile, with its sculptured brick turrets held together with plaster—were the equivalent of richly chased parade armor. They may have deterred some enemies from attacking, but would have crumbled at the first assault. The walls and towers of Montagnagna in the Veneto are among the most impressive in Europe, but the town changed hands 13 times in 10 years, through negligence or treachery, during the early-16th-century War of Cambrai. A few served well. The Crusaders sacked Byzantium in 1204, but, in 1453, a weakened garrison held an overwhelming Ottoman army at bay for weeks. Suleyman the Magnificent rebuilt the land wall, which has survived to this day, and is now being restored.

Torrechiara, a fairy-tale castle of the 15th-century near Parma, Italy [54]

(Left and below) The medieval walls of Montagnana in the Veneto look impressive, but were ineffective [55, 56]

Functional walls of Castelvecchio,
Verona, Italy (58)

Marostica, another Venetian dependency,
is now celebrated for its living chess game (59)

Kasbah of Taorirt at the edge of the Moroccan Sahara [57]

In general, city walls were expensive straitjackets—a necessary evil in times of unrest and a much-resented burden in peaceful eras. New taxes on residents and trade were unpopular, and this encouraged municipal authorities to build cheaply and skimp on maintenance. Social and economic controls often loomed larger than defense. However ineffective they may have been in a siege, walls allowed the authorities to charge tolls on incoming goods, and to monitor the movements of residents as well as strangers. The sergeants in charge of London's medieval gates were required to be 'skillful men, fluent of speech, to keep a good watch upon persons coming in and going out so that no evil might befall the city.'

Adobe walls surround the old city of Marrakesh, Morocco [60]

Gatehouses were leased out to generate income, and squatters were allowed to build against walls and within the space intended for the mustering of troops, thus compromising security and adding to the overcrowding within the gates. Monasteries, fairs, cemeteries and other functions were pushed outside, suburbs grew up around them, and the circuit of walls was enlarged to protect and control this growing population. The city plans of Moscow, Paris, and Istanbul show the successive circuits as clearly as the growth rings of a tree.

Ruined land wall of Istanbul, rebuilt by Suleyman after the Ottoman conquest in 1453 [61]

Water and mountains cost nothing to build or keep up. Shakespeare described England as:

'This precious stone set in a silver sea,

Which serves it in the office of a wall

Or as a moat defensive to a house,

Against the envy of less happier lands.'

Bodiam Castle, built in the 14th-century to deter French attacks on southern England [62]

(Right) Fragment of 12th-century city wall on the Rue Clovis in Paris [63]

The sea protected England from invasion by the Spanish in Shakespeare's day, and again from Napoleon and Hitler. But England was full of castles and fortified towns, especially along the Welsh border. Similarly, Venice was protected by its lagoon, but its rulers walled their possessions on the mainland. A massive sea wall defended the lagoon from erosion by the Adriatic; enemies may come and go, but the combat with nature is endless.

RESTE DE L'ENCEINTE
PHILIPPE AUGUSTE
XII SIÈCLE

Castles were feudal status symbols, but they were also the anti-missile emplacements of their day, reflecting the latest advances in military science. The Tower of London and Edward I's castles of Carnarfon and Conway were built before the introduction of cannon in the 15th-century. High stone walls, turrets and moats offered the best protection against scaling ladders and light missiles. From below, they looked impregnable and gave the defenders a psychological advantage. Such castles were often built to protect a city—though residents were expected to provide a first line of defense. In the samurai quarters of Japanese castle towns, stout garden walls along winding streets provided cover for defenders, who would leap out to ambush invaders.

Arrow slits in the White Tower (1097), Tower of London [04]

City wall and Minster, in York, England [65]

Pub built into the city wall of Southampton, England [66]

(Above and below) Carnarfon Castle, built by Edward I to enforce the English domination of Wales (67, 68)

Invaders were liable to be ambushed in the walled samurai quarter of Kanzawa, Japan [69]

Massive stone walls defend the Imperial Palace in Tokyo [70]

(Left and right) Himeji, the Castle of the White Eagle, Japan—a mix of fantasy and practicality [72, 73]

Star-shaped fortifications of Elvas,
which defended the Portuguese
border with Spain [71]

Artillery changed everything. In a flurry of treatises from the 16th-century on, artists and engineers (including Michelangelo and Leonardo) combined Renaissance symmetry with a new technology of defense. High, sheer curtain walls were replaced by an in-depth system of low, angled bulwarks of earth faced with stone which would resist bombardment and provide defenders with stable gun platforms and a clear field of fire. Walls were canted to deflect cannon balls; detached bastions sheltered the main circuit and kept attackers at a distance. The castle builders of Japan went in for show, but at the base they relied on massive, concave stone walls and sharp turns between a succession of gates. In Europe, star-shaped defenses became the new orthodoxy. Vauban, the 17th-century military engineer, ringed France with such fortifications. From above, or in the models displayed in the Musee des Plans en Relief at Les Invalides in Paris, they resemble the contemporary gardens of Le Notre. Here is the baroque obsession with radiating axes, the geometry of absolutism.

Long before Europe's tyrants were overthrown, their fortifications
had become an empty sham. Lucca and Antwerp were among the
first to landscape their ramparts. Louis XIV allowed Paris to create
promenades over obsolete city walls in 1636, introducing the word
'boulevard,' derived from *boulevart* (bastion), into the language.
By the end of the 18th-century, walls were useful only as a means
of regulating traffic and collecting customs dues, and they were
soon torn down to create linear parks and new arteries. Vienna's
Ringstrasse is the most spectacular of these.

A covered walkway runs atop the walls of Murten, Switzerland

Early Renaissance walls defended Lucca, Italy,
and now serve as a public promenade [74]

Gardens surround the circular wall of Nordlingen, Germany [76]

Grown-over fortifications of Palmanova, a Venetian 'ideal town' of 1593 [77]

Roman slate walls in the Galician city of Lugo, Spain [78]

Smaller, less expansive towns preserved their walls, while opening wide the gates—which had long been purely decorative. The Romantic Movement, which idealized the age of chivalry, cherished and restored its remains. Viollet-le-Duc put his stamp on Carcassonne, which now looks as inauthentic as a Disney castle. Restoration continues on the circuits around Avila and Toledo. In northern Italy, where many old towns have kept their walls, the effect is enhanced by decay. The bastions of Palmanova, once a model Renaissance city, have now been abandoned to sheep and vegetation.

The walls of Carcassonne, France, restored too well in the 19th-century by Viollet-le-Duc [79]

(Left and below)
The Ark (fortress) of Bukhara, devastated by the Bolsheviks, was recently rebuilt [80, 81]

European fortifications inspired other kinds of protective wall, even before the Romantics began to castellate their villas and civic monuments. In 1653, Dutch settlers in New Amsterdam paid a retired pirate to build a timber wall as protection against the Indians who had sold them Manhattan, and might one day want it back. The pirate pocketed half the money and used inferior timber, much of which was pilfered for firewood. The Indians never attacked, and the settlers surrendered to the British without a fight in 1664, leaving only Wall Street to mark their Maginot Line. None of Spain's settlements in Mexico required a wall, but everything within the town was enclosed, and battlemented walls surround many church forecourts—a fitting emblem for a militant religion. Dungeons were a feature of medieval castles, so it seemed appropriate to use the castle as a model for jails—when retribution, not reform was the goal. Richardson's Allegheny County Court House in Pittsburg suggests a fortress from which no inmate could ever escape.

Church atria, Cholula, Mexico [82]

Avila's 11th-century walls rest on Roman foundations [83]

Restored wall of Toledo, Spain [84]

Allegheny County Jail and Court House, Pittsburg, designed by H.H. Richardson, 1884–88 [85]

Materials

T he legendary modern architect Louis Kahn liked to converse with his materials, asking a brick, for instance, what it wanted to be. Few building blocks are treated with such consideration, but the beauty of walls derives much from the skilled and appropriate use of mud and brick, stone and timber, glass, steel, and shuttered concrete. Traditional cultures employ indigenous materials with innate artistry, making walls an expression of place and human creativity.

(Left and below)
Masonry bases of temples in
Kanazawa and Nikko, Japan [86, 87]

The long-lost Inca city of Machu Pichu, Peru [88]

Some of the most ancient and impressive walls were assembled from stones, often of great size, that were cut and fitted together without mortar. Few sights are more impressive than the long-lost city of Machu Pichu, high in the Peruvian Andes, where stone terraces ascend a mountainside like a great staircase leading to heaven. Throughout Peru, Inca walls have withstood centuries of earthquakes and neglect, with joints so tight that one cannot slip a knife between the stones. Japanese masons employed similar techniques for castles.
In Greek temples, iron clamps secured the marble blocks, which were hauled into position with ropes looped around projecting bosses. These were generally removed, but they can still be seen on unfinished parts of the Acropolis in Athens. Richard Meier mounted rough-textured blocks of travertine on a metal frame to create a massive base for the Getty Center in Los Angeles.

Hauling bosses on the marble blocks of the Propylae of the Acropolis in Athens [89]

(Left and above)
Travertine blocks suspended
on steel frames at the Getty
Center, Los Angeles [90, 91]

(Above and right)
Rocks in wire cages clad the Dominus
Winery, Yountville, California [92, 93]

Still more inventive was the outer skin that the Swiss
architects Herzog and de Meuron wrapped around
the steel and concrete Dominus winery in California's
Napa Valley. A grid of wire cages containing local
rocks turn a plain box into a dense architectural
sculpture, while providing a sun screen and a layer
of thermal insulation for the interiors.

Louis XIV described the Roman theater in Orange as 'the finest wall in my kingdom' [95]

Mortar allows masons to use a much wider variety of stones, in rough or finely dressed form. The ruined Anasazi pueblos in Chaco Canyon, New Mexico, are among the most impressive masonry structures in the Americas.

(Left and below)
Anasazi masonry in the Pueblo de Arroyo, Chaco, New Mexico [94, 96]

Roman brick, Norman and Saxon stones in a Winchester wall [97]

Straw boaters find
lodging in a flint wall
at Winchester school,
Britain [98]

In Winchester, a Roman city that later became
the capital of England, walls incorporate a
collage of historical fragments. Even the
poorest rocks can be concealed—as in the
sensuous white buildings of the Aegean—
or turned to advantage, as Frank Lloyd Wright
demonstrated at Taliesin West in Arizona.

(Left and above)
Whitewashed walls in the village
of Emporio, on the Greek island
of Santorini (99, 100)

Red rock wall at Roussillon in the Luberon region of France. (101)

Stones set in mortar at the medieval church in Lohja, Finland [100]

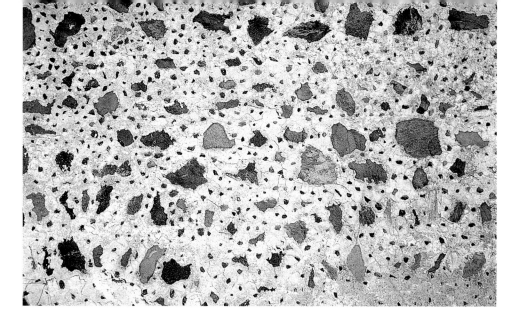

Stone orchard wall at Kampos, on the Greek island of Chios [104]

(Left and below)
Volcanic rock set in plaster at la Cave Village, Santorini [103, 105]

In contrast, Mies van der Rohe employed travertine alongside marble as an elegant veneer in his German Pavilion at the Barcelona exposition of 1929. The walls seem to glide past each other on the travertine podium.

(Above and right) Frank Lloyd Wright's 'desert masonry' at Taliesin West, Arizona [106,107]

I. M. Pei's East Building of National Gallery of Art,
Washington DC [108]

(Above and top right) Travertine- and marble-clad walls in Mies van der
Rohe's German Pavilion, Barcelona [109, 110]

Farm walls in Dingle, County Kerry, Ireland [111]

In the English Cotswolds village of Bibury, lichen covers a wall of limestone flats [112]

Retaining walls on the Mount of Olives, Jerusalem [113]

Farm walls define boundaries and retain terraces, confine livestock and protect them from harsh weather. They are found wherever stones are readily available, from the Mount of Olives to Martha's Vineyard. Drystone farm walls take their character from the shape and color of whatever materials are closest to hand. Limestone flats, fitted tightly together, have survived for centuries in the English Cotswolds. To the west, on Exmoor, sandstone is used in thin layers, and the walls are topped by jagged uprights to discourage trespassers. Irregular stones can be piled around an earth core and secured with thorn bushes. In Wales and the West of England, mortarless walls are called 'hedges,' in Ireland they are 'ditches,' and the craft of building them is still alive.

Farm walls on Martha's Vineyard, an island off Massachusetts [114]

In their superbly illustrated book, *Irish Walls*,
Alen MacWeeney and Richard Conniff cite an
estimate that the field walls of Ireland, put
end to end, would extend 240,000 miles—
that is, from the Earth to the Moon—though
one wonders who did the measuring. Circular
forts and shrines go back to the beginnings
of settlement; later, monks built impressive
bastions to protect themselves from Norse
raiders. Most farm walls were erected after
the 17th-century, when Anglo-Irish landowners
began making more productive use of their
holdings. As fertile commons were fenced, the
native Irish were compelled, often by force, to
scratch a living from stony soil. Family holdings
were constantly subdivided, for every square
foot counted in the struggle for survival.

Flying low over Inishmaan, a storm-wracked speck of land off Galway
Bay, one looks down on an intricate patchwork of gray and green.
To raise crops and pasture, livestock farmers cleared rocks from the
land and used them to create a network of walls that define tiny
fields and paths leading down to the beaches where seaweed was
gathered for fertilizer. It is a pattern that was established throughout
western Ireland before the potato famine of the 1840s decimated
the population and drove many of the survivors to America.
Limestone boulders and granite erratics left behind by glaciers
were stacked to create permeable walls that Atlantic gales could
penetrate; a solid structure would be flattened by the wind. There
are no gates; a farmer has only to remove a few stones to release
his cow from the field. Low passages permit sheep to pass through,
and projecting stones allow people to climb over.

(Above and right) Dry stone
walls in Lisdoonvarna and the
Burren, County Clare (115, 116)

(Above and below) Stone Age fort and farm walls on the island of Inishmaan, County Galway [117,118]

Some countries have too much stone and seek ways to use it up; others have none, and are driven to find inexpensive alternatives. Adobe (sun-dried mud) bricks are the material of choice in deserts, from the Sahara to the American South-West. In a technique that can be traced back to 5,000 BCE, blocks are made from moistened clay and sand, mixed with straw or dung to minimize cracking, and are shaped by hand or in a wooden form. In hot, arid climates they are cheap to make and easy to maintain, and their mass provides good thermal insulation. Cracked and crumbling or newly restored, the mud coating applied to these bricks assumes forms that are as fluid as the wind-molded dunes and mesas, and the protective surface can easily be renewed after winter rains.

Painted adobe walls at Al Ateuf in the M'zaab Valley of Algeria [119]

Adobe fort, Rancho Las Golondrinas, New Mexico [120]

Ranchos de Taos church, San Francisco, New Mexico [121]

Flat stones protect mud walls from erosion in this Saudi Arabian house [122]

It is estimated that a third of the world's population still lives in adobe or *pise* (rammed earth) dwellings. However, the depopulation of rural areas and the blind pursuit of progress have endangered this heritage. In Africa and Asia, traditional materials and techniques are being displaced by concrete, plastic, and corrugated metal. In New Mexico, cement plaster was applied to adobe churches in order to reduce maintenance. Not only did this create an unnatural surface but it trapped the water that filtered to the core, causing the adobe bricks to erode from within. Local communities are now undertaking restoration on a volunteer basis. The Aga Khan Trust and the Getty Conservation Institute are leading efforts to restore endangered monuments and foster an appreciation of vernacular traditions. The International Conference on the Conservation of Earthen Architecture brings specialists together to exchange ideas and share the latest research.

Morada (penitential chapel) at Abiqui, New Mexico [123]

Bricks fired in kilns have greater strength, versatility, and durability than adobe. First used by the Egyptians and Babylonians, they became a major building material in Rome. Augustus, who ruled as the first emperor (44–14 BCE), boasted of inheriting a city of brick and leaving it marble, but time has revealed what Augustus concealed: the superbly engineered brick structures beneath the marble veneers. Architect Rafael Moneo used thin Roman-style bricks for the grand arches and sheer walls of the museum that houses Roman artifacts in the Spanish city of Merida, reviving a design that had held sway throughout the Byzantine era and into the Middle Ages.

Crinkle-crankle walls at the University of Virginia, Charlottesville [124]

Roman-style brick in the vaults of Rafael Moneo's Roman Museum at Merida, Spain [125]

Brick walls of Domus Severiana on the Palatine Hill, Rome [126]

Curvilinear wall of brick in Eladio Dieste's church at Atlantida in Uruguay [127]

Northern Europe had a special fondness for brick, exploiting its variety of color and texture in churches, palaces, and public buildings. Lombardy and the Hanseatic trading towns along the Baltic led the way in the Middle Ages. Bricks were carried to Britain as ballast and soon became the favored building material there, and in the Netherlands, from where the taste spread to North America. Crinkle-crankle brick walls, a feature of traditional English gardens, are employed in Thomas Jefferson's University of Virginia at Charlottesville. Architect-engineer Eladi Dieste employed a similar form for the walls of his 1959 church at the workers' settlement of Atlantida in Uruguay.

Apse of Dieste's Collegio de Lourdes, an unfinished church in Montevideo, Uruguay [128]

Pine siding on Finnish Pavilion, Expo 92, Seville [129]

In the traditional half-timbered buildings of northern Europe, plaster is applied over wattle and daub within the exposed structural frame to create a pleasing geometry of dark ribs and light surfaces. It is a style that reached its apogee in medieval Germany and Tudor England. The first American settlers went back to an earlier tradition of rough-hewn log cabins in which the cracks are filled with plaster. Timber is Finland's most abundant commodity, and its builders have used it with a quiet confidence, exploiting the natural beauty of its grain. It was also the preferred material in Japan until the exhaustion of native forests and the escalation of labor costs made it prohibitively costly. One of the delights of the old quarters of Japanese cities is to see how inventively wood is used to screen and protect interiors from the bustle of narrow streets.

Half timbered house, Copenhagen[130]

Log cabin in Skansen outdoor folk museum, Stockholm[131]

Street facade of wood house on Hanami-kochi, Kyoto[132]

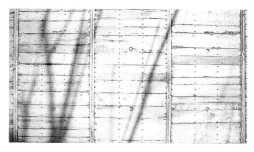
Shuttered concrete wall of Tessenkai Noh Theater, Tokyo [133]

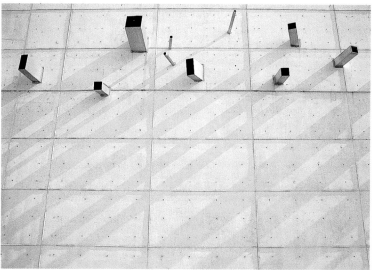
Antoine Predock's Museum of Science and Industry, Tampa, Florida [134]

Architect Hagy Belzberg protected a house in the California desert with this wall of tilted steel plates [135]

Polished concrete walls of Tadao Ando's Chapel of Light, Osaka [136]

The Japanese use concrete as creatively as they do natural materials. Drawing on their craft tradition, carpenters build forms from which the poured concrete emerges as a surface to rival stone. Tadao Ando exploits the play of light off grain-marked, or highly polished concrete to bring warmth and an organic feel to his austere volumes. A few European and American architects have followed his example, but have found it hard to match his level of refinement.

Mirror-glass Willis Faber Dumas offices by Norman Foster, Ipswich, Britain [138]

Glass curtain walls of Johnson & Burgee's Penzoil Building, Houston [137]

They have had more success with steel and glass, combining the strength and precision of the one with the transparency and reflectivity of the other to create curtain walls of extraordinary beauty. In the historic English town of Ipswich, Norman Foster wrapped a printing works with a mirrored wall that dematerializes the building by day, and reveals its inner secrets by night. The angled sheets of glass multiply the reflections and intensify the sense of place.

For the British pavilion at Expo 92 in Seville, Nicholas Grimshaw created a muscular steel and glass container that was shaded by a projecting roof canopy and cooled by water that flowed over the glass like a liquid skin. Richard Meier employs white enameled steel panels as cladding and a scaling device on the Platonic solids of his houses, museums, and civic buildings. Frank Gehry began using metals as an element in his architectural collages before using it as the sole material to wrap the expressive forms of art institutes in Toledo and Minneapolis, and creating a titanium-scaled sea monster that rises from the river in Bilbao to house the new Guggenheim Museum.

Eames House (1949), Pacific Palisades, California [139]

(Right)
Nicholas Grimshaw's British Pavilion, Expo 92, Seville [141]

Lead-coated copper clads Frank Gehry's Center for Visual Arts, Toledo, Ohio [140]

The only material limitation in building a wall is a lack of imagination. Bottles, beer cans, and even bones have been pressed into service. The late Grandma Prisbee, an eccentric collector, created structures of bottles, pencils and car headlights in her garden near Los Angeles. A lifetime of cans went into a railway worker's house and garden wall in Houston, Texas. Five thousand deceased monks supplied the raw materials for the walls of the 17th-century bone chapel in the church of Sao Francisco, in the old Portuguese town of Evora. The sight would have inspired Evelyn Waugh, the devout and misanthropic English novelist. In *The Brideshead Generation*, Humphrey Carpenter recounts how Waugh, bored by life in the country in the 1950s, occupied himself by building a semi-circular stone wall he called 'The Edifice,' advertised for human skulls to adorn it, and received a large number. 'Hideous' was the general verdict.

Grandma Prisbee's Bottle House, Simi Valley, California [142]

(Below and right) Beer Can House, Houston, Texas [143, 144]

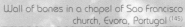
Wall of bones in a chapel of Sao Francisco
church, Évora, Portugal [(145)]

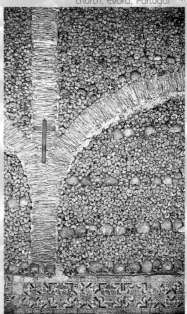

Ornament

The impulse to make a mark on a blank surface is universal and eternal. Too often it takes the form of graffiti, which are special only to their makers, and an eyesore for everyone else. Occasionally, as with the first cave paintings or the classic muralists, it is a work-of-art and a priceless record of an era. More commonly the overlay is pleasing but ephemeral, chipping and fading to become a shadow of its former self. Ornament can be organic or applied; created from the structural material or as a decorative overlay of plaster, marble, tile or paint that conceals the core.

(All images) Estate walls on Palmyra Street in Curnavaca, Mexico [(146-149)]

Fingos (faux marble) on a
wall in Pardes, Portugal [150]

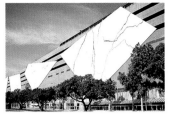

'Cracked' panels on Arquitectonica's
Miracle Center, Coral Gables,
Florida [151]

The simplest patterns are often
the most effective: 'diaper'
brickwork on an Elizabethan
country house, a similar cross-
hatching of tile and stone in Santa
Fe, or the zebra-striped cathedral
in Orvieto. Local specialties
include the geometric *sgraffito*
work of Pirgi on the Greek island
of Chios, masonry collages on the
estate walls Cuernavaca, and
fingos (faux marble) in the
Algarve region of Portugal.

Sgraffito pattern on church in Pirgi, Chios, Greece [152]

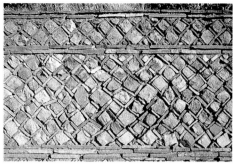

Diaper brick at The Vyne in Hampshire, a 16th-century English house [153]

A wall in Delphi inspired this design by David Bodelson at the Fenn Gallery, Santa Fe [154]

Zebra-striped stone chapels, Orvieto cathedral, Italy [155]

Romanesque brickwork on San Sepolcro chapel, Bologna, Italy [(156)]

Every region and culture uses materials in a distinctive way, and sometimes this tradition is enriched by artisans of rare skill—as in the marble and sandstone inlay of a Mughal tomb in Agra, or the baptistery of San Stefano in Bologna.

Slate-clad house in Limburg, Germany (157)

Relief pattern on a peasant house in the north of Rumania (158)

Farmhouse wall near Seoul, Korea (159)

Persian-influenced inlay at the Mausoleum of Itimad-ad-Daulah (1622) in Agra, India [160]

Bold relief patterns catch the light and add depth to a wall. Some of the most extraordinary are to be seen on the Ismael Samani mausoleum in Bukhara, a 35-foot cube of basket-woven brick with a shallow dome which was built over a thousand years ago. The Mongol conqueror Genghis Khan levelled the city in 1220, but the tomb had been buried, and it remained hidden until it was discovered by a Soviet archeologist in 1934.

Frieze on the palace of Darius I (ca. 518 BCE) at Persepolis, Iran [161]

The 10th-century Mausoleum of Ismael Samani in Bukhara, Uzbekistan [162]

Embossed plaster in the old city of Rhodes, Greece [163]

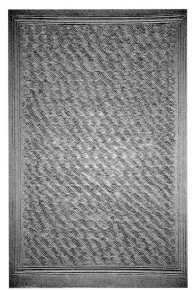

Traditional pargetting on a house at Lavenham in the English county of Suffolk [164]

Geometric reliefs at the pre-Columbian site of Mitla, Mexico [165]

Casa dos Bicos, Lisbon, Portugal [166]

The pre-Columbian temples of Mexico, the Casa de las Conchas (scallop shells) in Salamanca, and the less familiar Casa dos Bicos (diamond points) in Lisbon all demonstrate how the sun can add magic to the simplest reliefs.

Casa de las Conchas, Salamanca, Spain (105)

Fritz Hoger's Chilehaus, a prow-shaped office for a Hamburg trading company, is an Expressionist masterpiece in which the architect manipulates low-grade clinker bricks to masterly effect.

(Left and above)
Expressionist brickwork by Fritz Hoger, Hamburg, Germany [168, 169]

Cast concrete blocks in Frank Lloyd Wright's Millard House, Pasadena, California [170]

Brickwork in the courtyard of Alvar Aalto's summer house, Muuratsalo, Finland [171]

Other architects exploited the potential of the wall as a relief surface. Frank Lloyd Wright was inspired by Mayan temples in the houses he built in Los Angeles in the early 1920s, seeing them as models for a new kind of American architecture, much as Thomas Jefferson had found his inspiration for the fledgling republic in classical antiquity. The architect also wanted to ennoble lowly concrete by casting hollow blocks in patterned molds on site, and weaving them together with steel rods. Another great form-giver, Alvar Aalto, treated his summer home in central Finland as a laboratory in which he would try out building concepts; a brick collage in the courtyard was one of these experiments. Sam Rodia, a plasterer from Naples, created fantastically encrusted walls around his towers in Watts, California, and signed his work with the imprint of his tools in the wet mortar.

Imprint of Sam Rodia's tools on the walls surrounding his towers in Watts, Los Angeles [172]

Gold mosaic relief by David Sique

Rococo plaster figures adorn the facade of the Asam house, Munich [173]

rsity of Mexico [174]

Walls can take you by surprise. David Siqueiros turned a featureless block into a bold relief on the university campus in Mexico City. The Asam brothers employed a similar strategy on a plain house in Munich, adding a riot of rococo figures to echo those in the church they built next door and donated to the city. Marc Chagall thanked Evelyn Neff, his long-time Georgetown hostess, by presenting her with a 12-foot-wide mosaic that shines out from among the ivy on her garden wall.

Marc Chagall mosaic on ivy-clad wall in Georgetown, Washington DC [175]

Lou Dorfsman created a 60-foot-wide 'food wall' in the cafeteria of the New York headquarters of CBS, combining relief type that spelt out the names of foods with inserts of naturalistic fruit, vegetables and fish. Restoration work on the La Madeleine church in Paris was concealed by a realistically-painted pediment. In Vienna, Hundertwasser designed a block of public housing as a fantastic collage of painted surfaces, and a restaurant in lower Manhattan suddenly sprouted the Statue of Liberty's crown peering above a crazy-quilt facade. In other cities, a bricked-up picture frame, a flying nun, a huge bouquet, and an alligator delight the attentive stroller.

Trompe l'oeil painted facade concealed restoration work on La Madeleine church, Paris [176]

Lou Dorfsman's 'food wall' in the cafeteria of the CBS Building, New York [177]

Antoni Miralda's facade for the short-lived El Internacional restaurant, New York [178]

Color and ornament animate the Hundertwasser apartments, Vienna [179]

Enlivening a 17th-century brick wall in Amsterdam [180]

A nun passes through an old building in Budapest [181]

Brick reliefs on the Berlin zoo [182]

Flowers and a financial report on a wall near the Paris stock exchange [185]

Restored wall of the Dome of the Rock, Temple Mount, Jerusalem [184]

Tilework in the Shah-I-Zindeh, a 14th-century necropolis in Samarkand [185]

Islam brought the art of tiled walls to Iberia, from where it was carried to the New World. Naturalistic representation was forbidden by the Koran, and so a rich tradition of stylized texts, geometric patterns, and stylized flowers evolved, and mosque walls became as richly ornamented as oriental carpets. The fretted screen that admitted light and air but protected from the sun became a feature of Islamic architecture, and French architect Jean Nouvel picked up on this in his Institut du Monde Arabe in Paris. Light cells in the window walls control camera-like shutters that mimic the patterns of Islamic screen walls, and precisely regulate the level of sunlight passing through. Regrettably, the noise of the shutters disturbed scholars, and so they are now turned on just once a day.

Islamic-inspired shutters in the glass wall
of the Institut du Monde Arabe, Paris [186]

The Mexican city of Puebla resembles an outdoor ceramics gallery: every wall is richly patterned with tiles. The walls of the Temple of the Emerald Buddha in Bangkok contain gorgeously colored ceramic dragons to rival those of Gaudi in Barcelona. In London, tiles and terracotta appear as accents in the sober brick townscape, most dramatically on the Michelin Building, where tires bulge from the facade, and tiled panels recall the excitement of early auto races.

Tiled wall on the Avenida de la Reforma, Puebla, Mexico [187]

Ceramic relief in the Temple of the Emerald Buddha, Bangkok [188]

Azulejos in Sao Bento de Castris, Évora, Portugal [189]

NICE 1903
COUPE ROTHSCHILD

SERPOLLET

Racing at Nice in 1903: a faïence panel on the Michelin Building, London [190]

Walled port of Classe: a 6th-century mosaic in Sant'Apollinare Nuovo, Ravenna, Italy [191]

Garden wall of Sta Maria de Los Angeles, a mission on New York's Lower East Side [192]

The Byzantine brick churches of Ravenna contain golden mosaics, and something of that spectacle was captured in a church that rose, like a dazzling apparition, on New York's Lower East Side. Another great surprise is Frieda Kahlo's house in Mexico City: intensely blue on the street facade and containing, in the courtyard, a wall faced in volcanic rock and studded with conch shells.

Courtyard wall in the Frida Kahlo Museum, Mexico City [103]

Some painted walls are hidden away. A mysterious fresco of animals waiting on royal guests at an alfresco banquet was discovered behind the whitewash in a Zurich bookstore. Murals of feudal estates line the walls of the Golden Room in the fairytale castle of Torrechiara. A trompe l'oeil mural in a house in San Miguel de Allende and the interior of a Korean temple have a hallucinatory brilliance.

Painted interior of Korean temple [195]

Guillermo Rode mural in house, San Miguel de Allende, Mexico [194]

Fresco of castle in the Golden Room of Torrechiara, near Parma, Italy.[190]

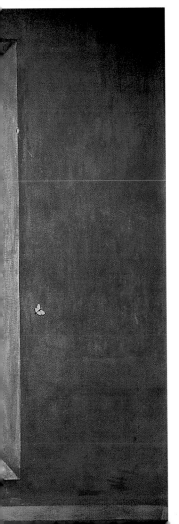

Fantastical 14th-century wall painting discovered in a Zurich book store [107]

Out of doors, art is vulnerable. A bespectacled
cow playing backgammon on a Vienna street
is still clear, but a fresco of Christ in Orta is fast
vanishing. Moslems who complete the Haj (an
obligatory pilgrimage to Mecca) celebrate the
fact on neighborhood walls, and as one such
inscription disappears another takes its place.

Cow playing backgammon:
a wall painting in Vienna [198]

Jesus and a neighbor in Orta, a lakeside town in northern Italy [199]

Antoni Tapies' mural on Catalan pavilion at Expo 92, Seville [201]

For artists, the challenge of murals is scale. What looks well on an easel may shrink to insignificance when applied to a three-story wall. Barbara Kruger successfully made the jump in a provocative artwork, 'Untitled (Questions),' she painted on the side of the Temporary Contemporary Museum in downtown Los Angeles. Antoni Tapies celebrated his native province in a spirited sketch that covered the facade of the Catalonian pavilion at Expo 92.

Barbara Kruger's Untitled (Questions) painted on the wall of MOCA, Los Angeles [202]

(Above and below) Richard Haas murals for the Architectural Center and on Milk Street, Boston [203, 204]

Richard Haas has specialized in *trompe l'oeil* murals that occupy the windowless side walls of buildings, transforming blank facades into architecture that contrasts with or echoes what is around the corner, and engages the passer-by. An architect, James Doman Jr, turned the street front of his building into a giant blueprint of his plan for its restoration.

Fanciful mural on West Broadway in Soho (205)

(Left and right) New York murals by Richard Haas on Soho and in Peak Slip (206, 208)

Blueprint for the remodeling of an architect's office
on East 22nd Street, New York [207]

In contrast to this tendency towards architectural abstraction, Los Angeles artists have veered towards surrealism. Les Grimes, who painted movie sets, began 'Hog Heaven' in 1957, disguising a meat-packing plant in east Los Angeles as a pastoral idyll. He fell to his death in 1968, and another Austrian immigrant, Arno Jordan, completed the project. The Los Angeles Fine Arts Squad was the catalyst for a lively program of murals that culminated in a publicly supported program for the 1984 Olympics. One of their first and best efforts was 'The Isle of California' which shows how the much feared 'Big One' might dislodge California and bring the Pacific Ocean to Arizona. Art imitates life: a somewhat less destructive earthquake struck soon after the mural was completed in 1971. Kent Twitchell emerged from the Squad to paint gigantic likenesses of Ed Ruscha, Lita Albuquerque, and other LA artists.

Murals of redwoods by Jane Golden in Santa Monica, California [209]

The Isle of California': an apocalyptic vision by the LA Fine Arts Squad [210]

(Above and opposite page) Los Angeles artist Kent Twitchell painting murals of Ed Ruscha and Lita Albuquerque [211, 213]

'Hog Heaven' on the Farmer John meat-packing plant in east Los Angeles [212]

Other cities participated in this explosion of mural art in the 1970s—an outgrowth of the spirit of rebellion and impatience with established values that characterized the Vietnam era. The Carl Solway Gallery of Cincinnati sponsored 'Urban Walls,' and, a decade later, the mayor's office in Paris organized a city-wide program with an elaborate map guide.

Latino murals in downtown Los Angeles [214]

(Right and below) Two of a series of early-1970s murals in Cincinnati [215, 216]

(Left and above) Trompe l'oeil murals in Toronto and Baltimore (217, 218)

Murals of the early 1980s on the Quai Branly, Paris (219)

Before the collapse of the wall, Berlin's Kreuzberg district was an unofficial outdoor gallery of angry and surreal artworks. Artists tricked the eye by adding an illusory third dimension. A giant pencil bursts through a flat wall in Montreux, a tree grew from an apartment building in Bern—and nature followed suit as roots and branches reached out in an octopus-like embrace of every wall within reach.

Leonardo da Vinci inspired this 1981 mural on a school building in Berlin [220]

Mural of theater scenery in Lyon, France [221]

Painted facade of Palazzo San Giorgio, Genoa [222]

Swiss trompe l'oeil mural, in Montreux [223]

(Opposite page) 'Zipper' (1978) by Gerd Neuhaus in the Charlottenburg district of Berlin [224]

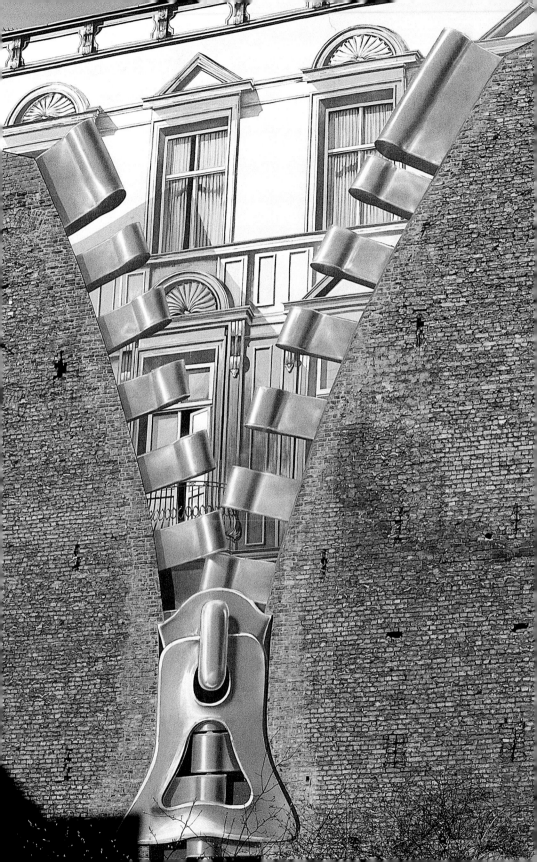

Plants enhance walls
in Seville (225)

Swiss trompe l'oeil mural, in Bern (226)

(Above and below) Nature takes over at Vizcaya in Coral Gables, Florida, and at La Antigua, Mexico [(227, 228)]

Color is a key element in walls that serve as blank canvases. In West African villages, women would repaint the walls each year in vibrant patterns of their own devising—a craft endangered by drought and the decline of tradition. Strong hues flourish wherever the sun has power, but especially around the Mediterranean and Caribbean and through Mexico. American photographer Deborah Turbeville commissioned a subtly layered blue facade for her house in San Miguel de Allende. Skilled painters applied seventeen coats and the client was thrilled until she heard neighbors remark that it was a promising start but they couldn't understand why she didn't complete it.

Molded and painted Hausa house wall, Zaria, Nigeria [229]

(Left and right) Downtown wall and Deborah Turbeville's house in San Miguel de Allende, Mexico [230, 232]

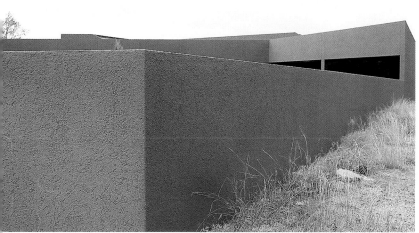

Building as billboard: Antoine Predock's Blood Bank in Albuquerque, New Mexico [231]

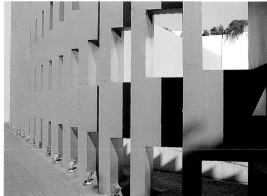

Ricardo Legorreta's Camino Real Hotel, Mexico City [233]

Lettering is another component of murals, harking back to the era before billboards, when every wall was an invitation to a signpainter. Walls also extend an invitation to play—to architects and amateurs alike. Charles Moore and friends delighted visitors to the 1984 New Orleans World's Fair with 'Wonderwall,' a shortlived fantasy structure surmounted by giant alligators.

Painted wall in Pioneer Square, Seattle [234]

Food sign in Tonantzintla, Mexico [235]

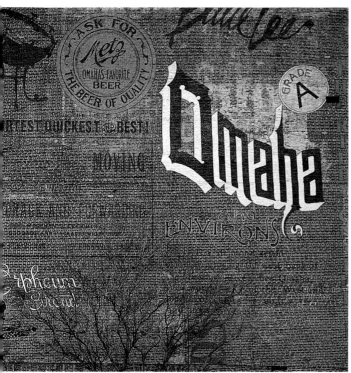

Sign mural of 1974 in Omaha, Nebraska [236]

Graffiti in Bucharest, Rumania [237]

Handprints in stucco on Scogin Elam Bray's Morrow Library, Atlanta [238]

Garden wall of a house in Pemberton, near Perth in Western Australia [239]

Charles Moore designed Wonderwall for the
1984 New Orleans World's Fair [240]

Time gives walls the patina of age. Colors fade, brick and stucco flake, one sign or poster peels to reveal a former occupant. Chance plays a role. When a building is demolished it may reveal a time capsule in the form of a period advertisement, its colors still pristine, or, more hauntingly, the hidden life of former occupants. In each case the product is what English artist John Piper called 'pleasing decay,' a melancholy reminder that everything changes and falls.

Artistically distressed facade in Carlton, Melbourne [241]

Crumbling houses in Clashmore, County Waterford, Ireland [242]

Hollywood wall the day after the 1994 earthquake [244]

(Left, above and top right) Mexican walls in picturesque decay: Guanajato and San Miguel de Allende [243, 245, 246]

Palimpsest of lettering at Rapp's Saloon, Santa Monica, California [(247)]

Wall advertisement of 1922 revealed by
demolition in West Hollywood, California [(248)]

Faded lettering of ca. 1930 in Weimar, Germany [249]

Chance and decay: exposed party wall
in lower Manhattan [250]

References

Selected Publications

Allport, Susan. *Sermons in Stone: The Stone Walls of New England and New York*, W.W. Norton, New York, 1990

Baker, B.G. *The Walls of Constantinople*, J. Milne, London, 1910

Big Art: Megamurals & Supergraphics. Environmental Communications, Running Press, Philadelphia, 1977

Dethier, Jean. *Down to Earth: Adobe Architecture— an Old Idea, a New Future*, Thames & Hudson, London, 1982

Gelb, Norman. *The Berlin Wall*, Michael Joseph, London,1986

The Geometry of Defence: Fortification Treatises and Manuals, 1500-1800, Canadian Centre for Architecture, Montreal, 1992

Jerome, John. *Stone Work*, Penguin Books, London, 1996

MacWeeney, Alen and Richard Conniff. *Irish Walls*, Stewart Tabori & Chang, New York,1986

Plumridge, Andrew and Wim Meulenkamp. *Brickwork: Architecture and Design*, Harry N. Abrams, New York, 1993

Quercioli, Mauro. *The Walls and Gates of Rome*, Newton Compton, Rome, 1982

Richmond, Ian Archibald. *The City Wall of Imperial Rome: an Account of its Architectural Development from Aurelian to Narses*, The Clarendon Press, Oxford, 1930

Runciman, Steven. *The Fall of Constantinople 1453,* Cambridge University Press, 1965

Safdie, Michal Ronnen. (photographs), *The Western Wall,* Hugh Lauter Levin Associates, Southport, Connecticut, 1997

Schaewen, Deidi von. (photographs), *Walls,* Thames & Hudson, London, 1977

Schuler, Stanley. *How to Build Fences, Gates, and Walls,* Macmillan, New York, 1976

Shimomura, Jun'ichi. *Meaning of Walls in Modern European Architecture,* Graphic-sha, Tokyo, 1984

Siren, Osvald. *The Walls and Gates of Peking,* John Lane, London,1924

Thomas, Avril. *The Walled Towns of Ireland,* Irish Academic Press, Blackrock, County Dublin, 1980

Thubron, Colin. *Behind the Wall: a Journey through China,* Heinemann, London, 1987

Turner, Hilary. *Town Defences in England and Wales: an Architectural and Documentary Study, AD 900–1500,* John Baker, London, 1970

Waldenburg, Hermann. (photographs), *The Berlin Wall,* Abbeville Press, New York, 1990

Acknowledgments

The authors would like to thank the many friends who have listened patiently as this book took shape over the past ten years, and especially those who have contributed ideas and photographs, including Katrin Adam, Stephen Antonakos, Steven Ehrlich, Gere Kavanaugh, Ken Kim, Michael Meredith, Patrick Macrory, Tim Street Porter, Fernando Vazquez, and Susan Venable. Special thanks to Shirley Sun for drawing the Chinese character for *cheng* (wall).

Photography credits

Katrin Adam: 192

Stephen Antonakos: 250

Hagy Belzberg: 135

Steven Ehrlich: 229

Alan Karchmer: 240

Gere Kavanaugh: 195

Patrick Macrory: 159

Michael C. Meredith: 6

Arnold Schwartzman: 1, 2, 7, 8, 13, 19, 21, 24, 25, 27–29, 35, 43, 44, 64, 89, 113, 130, 158, 177, 179, 181, 184, 198, 200, 223, 224, 237, 239, 244

Tim Street-Porter: 3

Michael Webb: 4, 5, 9–12, 14–18, 20, 22, 23, 26, 30–34, 36–42, 45–63, 65–88, 90–112, 114–129, 131–134, 136–157, 160–176, 178, 180, 182, 183, 185–191, 193, 194, 196, 197, 199, 201–222, 225–228, 230–236, 238, 241–243, 245–249